How to Book of Writing Skills

Letters, email, reports, resumes,

Author
J H Hood

ISBN 978-0-9875575-3-7

Description

Enhance and Improve Your English Skills: Learn How to Write Emails, Reports, Documents and More

Have you ever been frustrated by your boss constantly making changes to your documents? Annoyed at the time it takes to write something? Sick of sending emails that don't get read? Been asked to write a report and don't know where to start? Are people just not getting your message? Then this guide is for you!

In this guide you will find *practical and proven techniques* to write clearly, concisely and quickly.

Each section of the guide covers key points for writing well at work, including:

- the importance of identifying your audience, and then how to write for it
- using Plain English to get your message across
- how to structure your document
- the seven secrets to good email
- how to write sharp, accurate letters and memos
- how to use the simple tool of the mind map to improve your writing
- what to consider when you have been asked to write a report
- the key points of a resume, a cover letter and the job application
- getting on top of punctuation, spelling and confusing words

Good workplace writing is about getting a positive answer to the question: **Will your reader understand what you want them to know or do?** This guide will give you the skills to get that positive answer.

Dedication

To all those people who have and are still walking the learning journey with me—thank you a thousand times over.

May we continue the journey with joy in the challenges.

Contents

Introduction 5

Checklists 10

Basics of good writing 11

Planning for Writing 15

Mind Maps 17

Plain English & How to Make it Work for You 26

Punctuation & Spelling—Some Simple Rules 47

More Hints to Get Your Message Across 56

Writing letters and memos 60

The Report 66

Job Applications, Covering Letters and Resumes 73

The Seven Secrets to Good Email.................................81

Checklist 1—Planning for writing 95

Checklist 2—Improving your writing 96

Checklist 3—Writing good reports 98

Annex A: Confusing Words Exercise 102

Annex B: Email Subject Lines..106

Annex C: Example of a Good Email 108

Author Profile 111

Introduction

"It is better to light a candle than curse the darkness"
Chinese proverb

We can all write well

For many of us, the simple act of sitting down at a keyboard or a blank page changes us from a vital and competent person into a novice. We freeze, drag our feet, struggle— yet still end up turning in a job we're not happy with.

It doesn't need to be like that!

Most of the ways we have been taught to write lock us into patterns that don't work well for **everyday business writing**. These are patterns that we've learned at school, college or university—very effective for their purposes there...but not what you need for good writing in the workplace!

In this guide you will discover ways to counter those patterns as well as techniques to write well and quickly.

Plain English—also called Plain Language

The first pattern—we often think that when we write, we should use different, longer and more complex words than when we speak.
No, No, NO!

The Plain English—or Plain Language—Movement is a direct result of people being sick of complicated and formal writing, especially contracts and insurance documents. Plain English has now spread across the English speaking world, and the Movement is now into its thirties!

Business writing is about clarity, simplicity and good techniques—not about fancy or lengthy words. *Tell me what you want me to know or do, don't be long winded about it—and make it easy on the eye!*

Your reader will get your message clearly when you use Plain English techniques, those that focus on the audience and where you:

- use everyday English whenever possible
- use simple sentence structure—2 lines is long enough
- use headings and lists— direct the reader's eye and lead them through the document
- use tables—a picture tells a 1000 words
- explain technical terms if necessary
- use the active voice—'we did it', not 'it was done by us'
- use direct speech—'we will' not 'the organization shall'
- use lots of white space—the body language of the document

- are concise
- are positive—'when you send us the form we will...' not 'we cannot assist until you return the form'

One simple counter to the use of complex language is to read something aloud, and then ask yourself this question: *"If the person was sitting opposite me, would I say this to them?"* If the answer is *"No"*—then don't write it!

Another way to approach this and to stop yourself getting caught up in complex and confusing language is to imagine you had the person sitting with you, and then to write *what you would say to them.*

The key is not to translate the clear thoughts and words you have into gooblydook, usually because you think good writing must use long and complicated words.
You will get your message across when you understand that simple is best.

Reverse the Triangle

The second pattern—at school and during further formal study, we have been taught specific types of writing which are not the best ways of writing business letters, memos, reports or even emails.

There are four broad types of writing and each type requires different skills from us:
- **Academic:** to demonstrate knowledge, skills in analysis and reasoning

- **Evidentiary:** to tell the exact story as I experienced it—what I saw, heard, smelled
- **Literary:** Shakespeare, Milton, Dan Brown, Bryce Courtney, Tara Moss
- **Workplace:** to get things done

Most of us have been taught or learned the first three types—at school, at college or tech school or university, or through life's experience. But, and this is a big but, Workplace Writing requires different techniques...

In the two following pictures you can see a key difference between the type of writing most of us have learned—Academic—and what is required for good **Workplace** writing.

Academic writing has this structure:

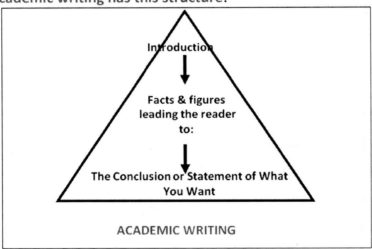

What you as the writer want from Day to Day writing is for someone to know or do something.

This is quite different from the usual outcomes required of academic writing, i.e. to demonstrate or describe new knowledge. So, in day to day writing, we need to reverse the triangle:

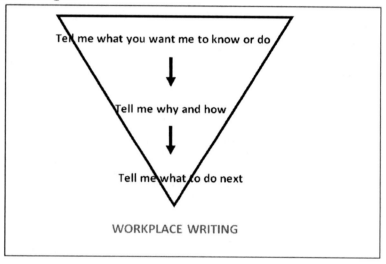

In this book, you will learn how to turn your written communication into a fluent, effective and satisfying process. You will understand how to:

- reverse the triangle
- plan what you want to say
- be clear about what you want your reader to know or do
- take less time to write your documents
- use Plain English

Checklists

There are checklists and examples included at the end of this tool—designed to help you improve the way you write.

You can use them in a variety of ways:
- when starting to write
- to understand your audience
- as you write

They are a powerful means of improving your writing skills—if you use them regularly.

Checklist 1—Planning for writing

Checklist 2—Improving your writing

Checklist 3—Report Writing

Example A—Email subject lines

Example B—Good email

Example C—Confusing words

Basics of good writing

*"Say all you have to say in the fewest possible words,
or your reader will be sure to skip them;
and in the plainest possible words
or he will certainly misunderstand them".*
        John Ruskin 1818–1900

All Good Writing starts well before your fingers reach the keyboard - it:

- is planned
- is written for the needs of the audience
- connects with and orientates the reader
- is appropriate for the context in which it will be read
- looks good - invites the reader to continue
- uses simple, active and positive language

And all effective writing has three major elements: purpose; audience; context.

Purpose

What do you want your readers to know or do? Tell them!
Make it clear—don't make them work hard to find out.
Beware the 'so what?' response.

Audience

It is not the writer's job to make things plain to everyone. It
is the writer's job to make things plain to the specifically
identified audience.

Consider:

- what does your audience already know?
- don't assume knowledge, but don't tell them again and again!
- how much do they need to know?
- don't give them detail they don't need—it will confuse them and add bulk to the text. But give them enough information to make a decision
- what will they understand? This is your area of expertise; is it theirs? Think about language: jargon, acronyms, tech-speak
- how will they respond to this sentence, paragraph or idea?

Context

There are two parts to Context:

1. People make sense of what they are reading by what comes before and what comes after, and what they already know about something; and
2. The environment in which the piece of writing will be read.

People look for patterns and logical flows in the way information is presented to them, and they look for links to information they already know.

The environment in which a document is read will affect the meaning the reader will take from it. For example, consider the impact if your document is read:

- with many other complex, possibly unrelated, reports
- with little or lots of time available
- briefly for general information
- thoroughly for detail
- to generate discussion
- with or without you there to provide supporting information or fill in gaps

We will explore each of these elements in the following chapters.
Pack your parachute and let's get started.

Planning for Writing

"Words are like spears: once they leave your lips they can never come back"
Benin proverb

Writing is like any other task—good planning improves your chances of succeeding.

The planning questions to ask yourself are:

- Why are you writing—what do you want to happen as a result of this interaction?
- Who is your audience?
- How will you communicate—for example a letter, an email a memo, a report?
- If appropriate, who should write, and who should sign, the communication?

The answers to these questions will start to shape your task.

Here are some other key issues to think of before you start writing...

Move Your Thinking

We often sit down to write with the focus of our thoughts on the document itself, and with words in our head like:

- I have to write this!
- How am I going to fit it in between all my other tasks?
- The boss always changes everything I write!
- What do I have to say?
-

We are concentrating on the immediate task of writing and the shape of the document in our own minds. What we need to do is to move our thinking to *"what do I want my reader to know or do?"*

People have many ways of planning the content—writing a list of key points or headings, doing a mind map, talking with colleagues—it doesn't matter how you plan...as long as you do plan.

Mind Maps

A Mind Map is a simple and effective way to start the process of writing letters, memos, job applications, manuals, policies or reports. It gets your information out of your head, to come up with other relevant details and to put it all together ready to write your document.

As you try the technique a few times, you will find it to be simple—it is as simple as it seems—quick and effective.

Tony Buzan, the inventor of the mind map calls the technique of mind mapping: "*The Swiss Army Knife for the brain*".

A mind map:

- is a way to capture ideas and information
- follows the way the brain works: links, jumps, connections, color, pictures
- should take only about 15 minutes

A mind map uses:

- associations and connections—you think of one thing that then makes you think of something else and so on...
- color and pictures
- curved lines

- a quick way of getting thoughts down - you don't lose them! Then you can organize them...

Get the words down without editing – do that once you have the first draft done

Creating a mind map is simple:

1. Draw a shape at the centre of a plain, unlined piece of paper. This can be just a circle or it can be a representation of the topic. Write the central idea or topic in the centre.

2. As you think of a main point, draw a branch from the centre.

3. Continue adding main points as you think of them. Identify each main branch with one or two words to give the main point—write the words horizontally, so that they can be read without needing to turn the paper.

4. Write quickly, without judging, editing or censoring—there will be time later to do that.

5. As you add each main branch, you will find that it helps you to think of other points—put them in... they can be new main points, or minor points.

6. Draw minor branches from the main branches. These are the minor points that need to be considered as part of each main point. Identify

these branches with one or two words—also written **horizontally**.

7. You can **add more** main branches and minor branches **at any point**—as your thinking progresses.

8. If you are able to, **draw in pictures** representing the points—this helps with free thinking and creativity.

9. Now, **sit back and look at the map**. Are there any common points that could be regrouped together, or are there other points or obvious gaps?

10. Make the changes—then **start writing your document**!

Here are some examples of mind maps:

This one is analyzing a problem, and the main branches are: cause, prevention, impact.

This next mind map is exploring love, with the main branches being dating, sex, romantic, family and wedding.

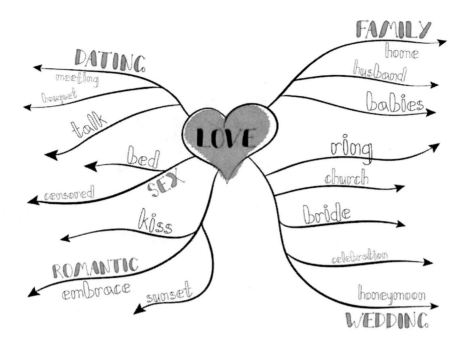

Here is another example!

Here is a mind map of a letter I wanted to write to a local college where I had attended a short course, and that I was unhappy about. The course content had not been as advertised, the lecturer was very poor, the room was badly set up and the handouts were dreadful. I wanted my money back!

PS: you don't need to be an artist!

So, this is the first mind map I drew:

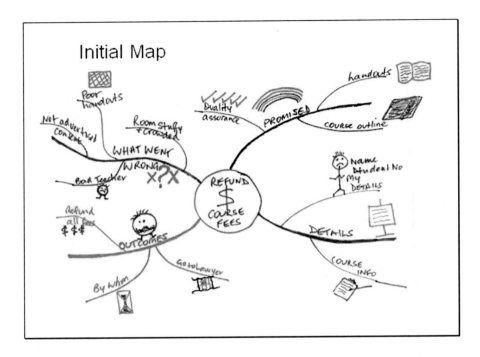

Initial Map

Then, I sat back and looked at it. I realized that I had left some points out, and maybe there was a wider solution than just: "my money back", so I re–drew the map:

As you look at the second map, you will notice:

- I have changed what I had written in the centre
- the range of possible outcomes has widened
- more details are added into several of the branches: the college would need those
- the unrealistic option of going to a lawyer has been changed to check out the college's grievance procedures

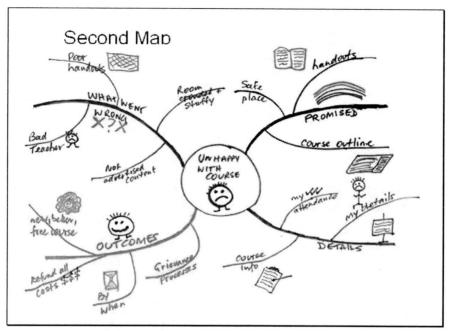

The whole process took me about 15 minutes.

Now I have a very clear plan of the letter I want to write, as well as the structure of the letter:

- each of the main branches is a heading
- each of the minor branches is a point to be made under its heading
- it is much simpler to decide what order each heading and point should go in

Another advantage of using a mind map is that it encourages you to start researching, thinking and writing at any point— rather than starting at the beginning, regardless.

You can also show your mind map to others for comment and input—it can be:

- a particularly useful way of making sure you have all the information you need
- a good way to get agreement from your boss about your document

If you are not sure what your main branches or headings might be, you can start with: *Who, What, Where, When, Cost and Risk*

Here is the letter I finally wrote based on my mind map:

My address

Date

Dear College Administrator,

Unsatisfactory Short Course—'WR 102: Writing for Online'

I attended your course 'WR 102: Writing for Online" in February this year, and found the course to be most unsatisfactory.

I request that you provide me with:

- either a full refund of the course fees and my parking expenses, or
- a replacement course of a much better standard, at no cost to me

---

> - The problems with the course were:
> - the content was not as had been advertised
> - the handouts were very poor
> - the room was crowded and stuffy
> - the lecturer had poor skills
>
> *My details are:*
>
> - Student number: XT 123456
> - I attended all sessions: 5, 8 and 12 February
> - fees paid: $135
> - parking costs: $30
>
> *Please respond to me by (a date two weeks from this letter).*
>
> *Yours sincerely,*

As you can see, the letter is very straightforward—the mind map has given me all the details and the order in which to put them.

There is a great deal of information about mind maps on the Internet, and some excellent free software if you prefer not to do your own drawings.

Use Checklist 1 to Plan your Writing

Plain English & How to Make it Work for You

"Rule 17: Omit needless words"
"The Elements of Style"
William Strunk

Good writers have been supporting the Plain English movement—in some countries also known as **Plain Language**—over the past 30 years. You may have seen some of the benefits yourself in the form of vastly improved contracts, insurance documents and the various levels of government communications.

Plain English (or Plain Language)

Plain English is writing that **works at** communicating with the reader. It is writing that:

- uses everyday English whenever possible
- uses simple sentence structure—2 lines is long enough
- uses headings and lists—directs the reader's eye and leads them through the document
- uses tables—a picture tells a 1000 words
- explains technical terms if necessary
- uses the active voice—*'we did it'*, not *'it was done by us'*

- uses direct speech—'we will' not 'the organization shall'
- uses lots of white space—the body language of the document
- is concise
- is positive—'... when you send us the form we will...' not '...we cannot assist until you return the form...'

Using Plain English demonstrates a respect for your audience and for yourself. Most importantly, it is not difficult to do—it just takes practice.

Start to unlock the secrets of good writing by using Plain English from now on!

For the reader, every document begins as a mystery.

What Do I Have To Do?

Your audience comes to your document asking 'Do I have to do anything? '

You must answer this question for the reader as early as possible—if you don't, then your reader will scan your document rather than read it—skipping your carefully organized ideas or arguments.

Asking this question is also an extremely good way of keeping yourself focused on what you really want—and need—to communicate. It is a good technique to write the answer to this question on a piece of paper and keep it visible as you write.

Regularly ask yourself: Does this piece of information progress the reader's understanding about what I want them to do?

You will find that it helps you to keep your writing simple and to leave out irrelevant information.

As you reveal the content, your reader will make sense of each item based on:

- what comes before
- what follows, and
- what they already know about the subject

Write your document to **unfold your writing** so that your reader has a context from which to read and understand. Find links with the reader's previous knowledge and experience, or with previous correspondence.

Give your reader **sign posts**. You can do this by using headings from the start of the document, or, if there has been previous communication—make reference to that up front, for example *'Following on from...* 'or *'In reference to...* '

Getting Started

So how do you **get started** on your document?

First—settle these points:

- are there any **organizational conventions** about layout, wording or tone that you need to follow? How will you find them?
- what do you know about the topic? Do you have all the

information you need?
Where and how will you get
it?

- how will you plan the
  content? Will you start with
  a list of key points, or a mind
  map?
- how will you structure the
  document? Will it be a
  memo, letter, report, email,
  or ...?
- what point or topic will you
  start with? What next? (You
  don't have to start at the
  beginning—it's okay to start
  anywhere and write in any
  order—just make sure you
  pull it all together at the end
  to make sense)

People have many ways of planning the content—writing a
list of key points or headings, doing a mind map, talking with
colleagues—it doesn't matter how you plan...as long as you
plan.

Use your mind map.

Now, get writing! Don't try for perfection—just get some
words down.

Don't just sit there staring at a blank screen or piece of
paper. Don't try and get the perfect words down at once.
Don't concentrate on how much you have yet to write and
build mountains in your mind.

Try some of these techniques:

- jot down some dot points
- allow yourself to write rough notes or a draft
- write what you can right now for the section you are working on, then move to another
- give yourself short breaks between sections—time to think. This will enable you to review and rewrite

You can always change it...most people do...just get something down and the rest will follow.

Good writers usually write a draft the first time they work with a particular topic or for complex documents. This is very sensible—not an admission of failure!

What Would You Say?

If words are hard to find, then imagine that you are sitting opposite the person you are writing to, and ask yourself *"What would I say to them?"* This will usually force you to be clearer in what you write.

How Readers Read

There is a **natural** rhythm to reading.

Your reader will usually:

- pay more attention to the first part of the document
- pay less attention to the middle of the document
- refocus toward the end

Readers scan or skim the document, looking for what you want them to do, for key points and summaries, or for the specific pieces of information that are relevant to them. They will become bogged down in long paragraphs and long sentences.

They may be confused if the flow doesn't follow a natural order, such as *chronological, levels of importance* or *themes*.

A good technique for testing readability is to read it out aloud. If it flows well in speech, this is a good sign. It does not mean that you should write as you speak! Rather, as you read, listen for the flow and sound of the document— is it clear and easy to read?

If, as you read aloud, you find yourself using words and technical terms that you would not say to someone sitting beside you, then don't write them!

Body Language

The way the message is delivered is as important as the words.

In face to face communication, people take only about 10% of the meaning from the words that are used. Over 50% is read from body language, while the remaining 30% to 40% comes from the tone of voice.

We believe the body language, not the words!

Any written communication has its own body language. The look of the document can either:

- encourage the reader to read on, or
- set up blocks to successful communication

Factors such as layout, spelling, punctuation, grammar and tone are part of the body language of the document.

Imagine a densely written page, with long paragraphs, complex words, and with no headings or lists...this document is saying 'I'm *a complicated, difficult, hard document...and I'm not interested in sharing my content with you... '*

Now imagine a document with short paragraphs, headings, lists and plenty of white space...this document is saying *'I want you to read me, I'm open and comprehensible and I want to share my information with you... '*

Similarly, a document filled with unfamiliar jargon is immediately saying to your reader 'I'm *not really interested in you understanding this document...'*

Direct the Reader's Eye

A document will be easier to read if you direct the reader's eye. You can do this by:

- having plenty of white space in the document—use good margins, bulleted lists, spacing between paragraphs and a variety of formatting techniques
- using short sentences and paragraphs
- using sign posts—headings and sub-headings
- using consistent fonts and font sizes except for emphasis
- leaving the right margin uneven rather than justified—it is easier for the eye to follow an uneven margin

Use Tables

Tables are a good formatting technique—and you can use them in formal as well as informal documents. They are useful when you:

- present complex information
- give instructions
- make comparisons

Here are two examples of using a table:

Example 1. Instructions to change a password

On 15 April, <u>everyone</u> will need to do the following:

Steps	Action
1	Log onto the system
2	Enter your current password
3	Change your password to a new one with at least 8 characters— consisting of six letters and 2 numbers

Example 2: Instructions about using software

If you need to acquire new software:

Do	Don't
Get ALL your software from Company staff	Don't use unauthorised software
If you spot signs of physical tampering, return the package to the supplier	Don't use software with opened packaging

Note: In the 'Don't' column, always repeat the word **don't** in each cell...people **read** quickly and often miss which column they're reading.

Use Lists

Lists, both bulleted and numbered, make information easier to work with.

Read the following paragraph:

'When writing a report, consider what, why, how, who and where: why you are writing it, what the topic is about; what you already know about it; who else might know about it; where might you find information about it and how you make sure you are covering all the information. '

Now, look at the same information shown in a list:

'When writing a report, consider why, what, who, where and how:

- Why are you writing it?
- What is the topic about?
- What do you already know about it?
- Who else might know about it?
- Where might there be information about it?
- How do you make sure you are covering all the information? '

The list is much easier to read—and to remember!

Try Different Fonts

Use **different fonts and formatting** to make something important stand out:

- make it bigger
- use italics
- put extra space around it
- use a different font or color
- use bold
- use an indent or a separate line

use a table	

But—beware—like any technique, <u>overuse</u> defeats the original intention.

Used well, these techniques will lead the eye gently across the page—but too many tables or lists make the eye jump from space to space, and make the page look busy.

Active Voice

Wherever possible, **bring your writing to life by using the active voice.**

The passive voice distracts your reader and slows them down, and it can lead to ambiguity and confusion.

In the following table you can see the improvement when the active voice is used.

Passive	Active
Security shall be provided at the courthouse	*(Who will provide the security—you or us?)* We will provide security at the courthouse
It is hoped by both parties that further delays can be avoided	Both parties hope to avoid delays
The privacy of the applicant will be respected in the review process	We will respect your privacy
Smoking is prohibited outside the entry doors	Please don't smoke outside the entry doors Please don't smoke here
All communities shall be consulted prior to a decision being made	We will consult with you before we make a decision

Use "You"

Your communication will be far more effective if you use the first person: *I* and *you,* rather than the third person, disembodied voice: *it is recommended... the preferred approach is...*

Which of the following would you prefer to read?

Passive	Active
Interested parties should respond to this notice electronically to indicate individual willingness to participate in the experiment	If you would like to participate, please fill out the attachment and email it to ...

And which of those examples would you actually say to someone?

'*You*' reinforces the message that the document is intended for your reader. Similarly, using '*we*' to refer to your organization brings you closer to your reader and improves the communication.

One Idea per Sentence

Express only one idea in each sentence.

Long, complicated sentences often mean that you aren't clear about what you want to say. Shorter sentences show clear thinking.

Shorter sentences are also better for conveying complex information—they break the information up into smaller, easier-to-process units.

Try and keep your sentences down to two lines!

Simplify, Simplify, Simplify

"Never use a long word where a short one will do...
...If it is possible to cut a word out, always cut it out...
... Never use the passive where you can use the active..."
"Politics and the English Language", 1946 George Orwell

Focus on the key points—keep the language and style simple and straightforward.

It is very easy to slip into using highly technical or formal language—especially if you know the topic well, or it is highly complex. This can often be an indicator that you are really writing for yourself rather than your audience.

The challenge is to simplify your language—**cut out formal, complex and unnecessary words and phrases**. For example, look in the following lists:

Unnecessary Words & Phrases

Instead of:
A survey of volunteers in regional locations was conducted
Try:
We surveyed regional volunteers

Instead of:
They came to the conclusion that
Try:
They concluded

Instead of:
We made the decision to
Try:
We decided

Instead of:
in consideration of the fact that
in light of the fact that
in view of the fact that
Try:
because

Instead of:
henceforth
Try:
from now on

Instead of:
herein enclosed is
Try:
I have enclosed

Instead of:
pursuant
Try:
as we agreed, as a follow up

Instead of:
Written notification shall be made to this office in the event that ownership has been transferred
Try:
You must notify us in writing if you transfer ownership

Note: Look at how much clearer the above list would be if set out in a table!

Unnecessary Words & Phrases	
Instead of:	**Try:**
A survey of volunteers in regional locations was conducted	We surveyed regional volunteers
They came to the conclusion that	They concluded

Jargon

Unless you are certain that your audience will understand the jargon and technical terms you are using—don't use them!

It is very easy to slip into bad habits around jargon, and to make assumptions about what your reader will know. Another trap we can fall into by using unnecessary jargon is that we can lose sight of the real meaning and create meaningless euphemisms.

Consider the following examples:

Instead of:	Try
Please execute this document	Please sign this document
We had a negative patient care outcome	The patient died
We need to gain traction on this project	We need get moving on this project
We are going through a down–sizing operation	We are reducing the number of employees

Instead of
We need to make sure of the social inclusion aspects of this program
Try:
We need to make sure that this program improves client's ability to take part in the community

Instead of:

Grading activity required by new development would have associated short-term erosion impacts.
Try:
Grading would cause soil to erode.

Instead of:
We must have measurable milestones for this plan
Try:
We must have targets identified in advance as part of this plan so that we can measure its success

Note: Look at how much clearer the above list would be if set out in a table!

Jargon	
Instead of:	**Try:**
Please execute this document	Please sign this document
We had a negative patient care outcome	The patient died
We need to gain traction on this project	We need to get moving on this project

Acronyms

Acronyms are abbreviations, made up from the initial letters or phrases of a descriptive phrase, which form words usually able to be pronounced.

Many acronyms are well known, for example:
CEO—**C**hief **E**xecutive **O**fficer
AA—**A**lcoholics **A**nonymous

NATO—**N**orth **A**tlantic **T**reaty **O**rganization
BBC—**B**ritish **B**roadcasting **C**orporation
NASA—**N**ational **A**eronautics and **S**pace **A**dministration
ICS—**I**ndian **C**ivil **S**ervice
Laser—**l**ight **a**mplification by the **s**timulated **e**mission of **r**adiation
DNA—**d**eoxyribo**n**ucleic **a**cid
AIDS—**A**cquired **I**mmune **D**efinition **S**yndrome
Aka—**A**lso **k**nown **a**s

Acronyms can be a useful means of simplifying your writing—provided that:

1.   You explain them the first time you use them in your document, i.e. *South Australia (SA), one of seven regions of Australia* , and
2.   You are certain that your reader will understand them, i.e. *ABS (anti-lock braking system).*

While many acronyms are in common use and understood by most readers, this is not always the case. Here are just a few of the possible meanings of **DA**:

Algerian Dinar	Database Administration	Date	Decision Analysis
Delegated Authority	Denmark	Department of Agriculture	Department of the Army
Devil's Advocate	Direct Action	Directory Assistance	District Attorney
Dopamine	Double agent	Drug Abuse	Drugs Anonymous

Use acronyms with care!

Use Inclusive Language

It is a poor communicator who excludes a part of their audience by the language or communication methods they use.

Does your language exclude anyone or any group such as older people, people from a particular culture or location, people with a disability or people from one gender?

When you identify your audience and their needs, you will become aware of any particular sensitivities and issues. This will give you the opportunity to address these early in your communication process.

For example, 'Every *staff member must bring his ID to the meeting '*
could become:

'Every staff member must bring their ID to the meeting '

or, much better

'Please bring your ID to the next staff meeting '

Other techniques are:
- describing **what the person does** instead of using the title, e.g. *the person chairing the meeting*
- using **neutral** terms like *'police officer'* instead of *'policeman'*

Questions & Answers

Each document is a mystery to your reader—the reader comes to your document with questions.

For some types of document, anticipating these questions and using a question and answer format can be very effective. This can be in the form of an FAQ—Frequently Asked Questions—section.

This is particularly so:

- when you are advising the reader of changes to a process or program
- for instructions
- to make possible consequences crystal clear

Tables are particularly good for this, for example:

Action or Issue	What to do
Applying for a new ticket	Get Form 123 from (address or URL), & post to …
Applying for an aged concession	Get Form 456 from (address or URL), & post to …
Reporting a lost ticket	Get Form 789 from (address or URL), & post to …

Punctuation & Spelling—Some Simple Rules

"When I use a word, it means what I chose it to mean—neither more nor less"
   Humpty Dumpty—Lewis Carroll

Rule 1—Less is best—read aloud
Rule 2—Use a *Style Manual* or *Guide*
Rule 3—Be careful when using spelling software

Punctuation and Spelling have ways of confusing all of us at some time. The path to success is:

- practice and observation
- co–opt a good proof reader to help you: spell checking software will tell you the word is spelled right, but not if it is the right word—*'ewe'* & *'you'*; *'the n'* & *'then'*
- use a good Dictionary or Style Guide
- learn to use the *AutoFormat* function on your word-processing software

Punctuation

Keep it simple.

Commas (,):

- indicate a brief pause
- separate a statement from a question
- can replace *and, or, yet* or *but* in a sentence
- separate contrasting parts of a sentence or separate items

Colons (:):

- introduce a word, a phrase, a sentence, a quotation or a list
- can emphasize whatever is placed after them

Semicolons (;):

- separate items in a list where the items already contain commas
- connect to separate, but related sentences where an adjoining word has been left out

Brackets ( ):

- identify the abbreviation of a term that is going to be used often in a document, the first time it is used, i.e. *"Australian Tax Office (ATO)"* Then use *'ATO'* throughout the rest of the document

- define the meaning of an acronym, e.g. NASA (National Aeronautics and Space Administration)
- enclose information that expands on a statement you have just written, but is not essential, i.e. *"The football team has won several recent premierships (in 2002, 2003 and 2005) and could be well worth sponsorship"*. The question to ask yourself as you write is "How does this piece of information add value? If it doesn't, then leave it out!! *"The football team has won several recent premierships and could be well worth sponsorship"* is simpler and conveys the same meaning

Spelling or 'spelink'

Unfortunately first impressions do count and we do judge by appearance. So, it is important that you get your spelling correct.

It is also important that you don't allow spelling problems to stop you writing.
You can sort the spelling out once you have got your ideas down.

So what are some ways to improve your spelling? Well, there are a number of ways to try:

- get and use a dictionary
- read, read, read—the more you read, the better your spelling will get. Read <u>anything</u> that interests you—newspapers, magazines, fiction or non-fiction—and if possible, write down and memorize words that interest you
- make a deal with someone else who is a good speller to proof read your writing—you will surely be able to find something you are good at to do for them in exchange
- if you use a word processing software package, find out how to use the AutoFormat function, and put the common words you misspell or mistype into it
- don't get discouraged!

English changes over time: words are added, words fall out of favor and different countries spell words differently, for example:

- a new word - *'googled'* meaning to search for something
- a changed word - *'an invite"* instead of *'an invitation'*
- different countries - *'favoured'* (Australian/English) and *'favored'* (American/English)
- unused words - *'quoth'* is now *'said'*
- the whole new language of texting or SMS - *'ur lat8'* for *'you are late'*

Apostrophes (')

Many people are not sure where and when to use apostrophes.

Basically, there are two places when an apostrophe is appropriate:

1. When two words have been joined together and some letters have been left out, i.e. "*It's* time to go" for "*It is* time to go"; "*You're* late today" for "*You are* late today"; *They're* too late to enter" for "*They are* too late to enter".

2. Where you need to show the possessive—to show who owns what, i.e. "*The cat scratched the dog's nose*" for "*The cat scratched the nose of the dog*"

Confusing Words

Along with Apostrophes, there are some words in English that are easy to confuse. Here are some of them:

To, Too, Two

- To: part of a doing word: "They went **to** the garden **to** dig".
- Too: very, as well: "I was **too** late to get in. I was tired, **too**".
- Two: the number 2: "**Two** dogs chased the ball".

Your, You're

- **Your**: is a belonging word: "***Your** shoes are untied"*, i.e. the shoes belong to you.
- **You're**: short form of <u>you</u> <u>are</u>: "**You're** walking around with your shoes untied.

Their, There

- **Their**: is a belonging word: "*They put on **their** shoes"*, i.e. the shoes belong to them.

- **There**: shows place: "My shoes are over **there** in the cupboard ".

"Their" has also changed its meaning in the past ten years. It used to be used only as a plural word, for more than one person, but it is now used instead of *His* or *Her*, i.e. we used to write *"Everyone must **bring his or her** notebook"* now we generally write *"Everyone must bring **their** notebooks"*.

Accept, Except

- **accept**: a doing word, to receive or to agree: *"He **accepted** their praise graciously"*.
- **except**: Prepositions are words that specify place, direction, and time, meaning all but, other than:" *Everyone went to the party **except** Jo"*.

Affect, Effect

- **affect**: a doing word meaning to influence:" Will lack of sleep **affect** your exam results"?
- **effect**: a noun meaning consequence:" Will wearing poorly fitting shoes have an **effect** on your game?", and
- **effect**: a doing word meaning to bring about, to accomplish:" Our complaints

have effected a change in
the way the company does
business".

Advise, Advice

- **advise**: a doing word that
  means to recommend,
  suggest, or encourage:" *I
  advise you to be careful"*.
- **advice**: noun that means an
  opinion or recommendation
  about what could or should
  be done:" *I'd like to ask for
  your **advice** about this offer"*.

Split Infinitives

Some people fiercely dislike split infinitives; many others
find them merely slightly distracting.

Split infinitives occur when additional words are included
between *to* and *the verb* in an infinitive.

They may lead to confusion in what is actually meant. For
example, from "He decided *to* promptly *return* the money
he found", you could draw each of the following meanings:

- He **promptly decided** to
  return the money he found.
- He decided to return the
  money he found promptly.

They also can lead to cumbersome or awkward writing, for
example:

Split	Better
to quickly leave	to leave quickly
to always want	to want always
to easily excel	to excel easily
You fail completely to recognise	You fail to completely recognise
I like to on a nice day walk in the woods	On a nice day, I like to walk in the woods
The time has come to once again discuss our annual office party	Once again, the time has come to discuss our annual office party

On the other hand, they can add color and emphasis to a phrase "...*to boldly go where no-one has gone before...*"

Use Checklist 2—Improving Your Writing

Try the Confusing Words Exercise at Annex A

More Hints to Get Your Message Across

If you are writing for an organization, or to a large audience, it is worth considering these other factors that can impact on your writing.

Checkout the Filters

We all filter messages through our own perceptions, contexts and needs, and these affect the ways in which we send and receive all communication.

You need to take this filtering into account. Ways to do this are to develop your skills in:
- listening and clarifying
- anticipating problems and difficulties
- understanding the other person—sharing perceptions and needs
- keeping your message simple
- setting up ways of getting open feedback

Which Medium?

The kind of **writing**—or medium—you use, such as a letter, report, email, minutes of a meeting or a presentation, affects the way in which the message is received.

Each has its own impact—both advantages and disadvantages—on your audience. Your audience's access to, and use of, the medium is crucial, for example:

- the informality of a note or memo may change the perception of the importance you intended for a topic
- sending a time-urgent email is pointless if the audience has only limited access to computers
- formal meeting minutes or presentations may be less likely to produce creative input or open feedback
- a casual letter may be effective in some situations or cultures, while in others it may be inappropriate

Who Needs the Information?

It is okay for people to receive information in different forms, and in differing detail—according to their needs. But—all the people don't need all of the information!

Don't tell everyone everything! We only need to receive the information that is relevant to us at that moment. Not only are many people simply overloaded with information, but often we get lost in too much unnecessary information.

Similarly, a complex technical report may be appropriate for a project leader, while a tightly written executive summary may be more useful to a busy manager—and more likely to be read.

A verbal update might be appropriate for your team; a community group could need a presentation of the issues and options.

In the same way, each audience may have quite different needs as to when, and how often, they receive your communication.

The key is to understand the needs of each of your audiences and then to **be consistent** in how you communicate with them.

Repeat Key Messages

People often need to receive your message a number of times and in a range of ways before they understand, or before they are ready to pay attention. Take some time to work out the essence of your message, and then repeat it.

It is useful to integrate important messages into regular and routine communication channels— using different ways and forums, and different timing.

For example, a message about security or a new priority might appear on staff meeting agendas, at managers' meetings, as well as in staff newsletters and on internal emails.

Keep the Chain Short

The more people involved in the communication chain, the higher the likelihood of confusion and errors—keep the communication chain short.

Choose types of communication that will bring you as close as possible to your audience.

This may mean that you need to use more than one way or forum for communicating, for example, a memo, a newsletter article and a meeting, or a large presentation— each for different audiences.

Use Existing Means

People regularly use the communication channels that work for them, and the way you usually communicate might not be how your audience communicates.

Your communication will work better if you can discover and use the natural communication flows of your audience rather than cutting across them. In most instances, you will find that using existing communication means is most effective.

A good example of this is writing an article for a group's newsletter rather than sending them a formal letter.

Writing letters and memos

*"I didn't have time to write a short letter,
so I wrote a long one instead"*
Mark Twain

Letters

There are three key points to understand about writing letters:

1. People dislike long letters
2. You must give me a reason to read your letter!
3. Use Plain English

It is good practice to plan your letter; make a short list of your points, or use a mind map.

As part of your plan, always write yourself a statement of *"What I want the reader to know or do as a result of this letter"*. This will:

- keep your writing focused, and
- enable you to decide what to keep in and what to leave out, i.e. *'how does this piece of information add value?'*

The Greeting will depend on your relationship with the reader:

- if you are on 'first name' terms with the reader, use 'Dear Anne'
- otherwise use 'Dear Mr Purple', 'Dear Miss Green'
- if you are writing to a woman and don't know which title she prefers, use 'Dear Ms Green'
- if you don't know the person's name, use 'Dear Sir', 'Dear Madam' or occasionally 'Dear Sir or Madam'

You need to orientate your reader, to give them a context to read from—the reason for writing. You can do this in a number of ways, for example, start your letter with:

1. A heading, for example:
"Request for Renewal of License" or
"Refund of Fees" or
"Diabetes Testing"

2. An introductory sentence, for example:

"Regarding your request for renewal of license…",
or
"Thank you for your letter of 30 July, about refund of fees"
or
"Free diabetes testing is now available

Your first paragraph must then tell your reader what you want them to know or do. If you don't, then:

- the reader will simply skim the letter until they find that information, ignoring the detail or points you have written, or
- if the letter is too long, or your writing is too complex— they will stop reading

Here are some examples of first paragraphs that fit the headings and introductory sentences in the previous paragraph:

"To renew your license, you must fill in the form 123 and return it, with the fee of $25 to your nearest Office",
or
"We can refund your fees if you provide your receipt, and a doctor's letter covering the period of the course you missed"
or
"To book your place on the free Diabetes testing on 3 March, please call..."

As soon as your reader reads those words, they can see what it is you want them to know or do. You can now go onto the middle—with the attention of your reader.

The middle will be your points, answers and questions in a logical order. It is okay to use headings (not all capitals), bold text, bullet points and tables.

Keep your letter short and simple—people prefer to read letters that are less than two pages long. And they won't read them at all if you don't tell them in the first paragraph what you want them to know and do!

Each paragraph should address just one issue, and be no more than three or four sentences long.

If you need to include complex information, additional documents or legal technicalities, then put it in an Enclosure or Attachment—the name varies, but basically it is a place to put detailed information instead of cluttering up the body of your letter.

Give each Enclosure or Attachment a title, and if there is more than one, number them. You must make it easy for the reader to find the information.

The end does not normally need to be a summary. A suitable final sentence might be *'I hope this has answered your questions'*, *'Thank you for your help'* or *'If you have any questions, please ring...'*

Make sure that your letter clearly says who the reader should contact and how, and what they need to do next, usually with telephone number and email and a date.

The Sign off can be:

- *Yours faithfully*—if you don't know the name of the person you're writing to
- *Yours sincerely*—if you know the name of the person you're writing to
- *Regards*—if the person is a close business contact or friend

Some organizations and companies will have a standard format that you need to discover and use.

Collect copies of good letters and use them as starting points for your letters.

Memos (Memoranda)

Memos are basically letters written in a specific format for an organization or company.

Usually, they are internal documents, although sometimes they may be passed between various parts of large organizations such as multi–national companies, Government bodies and Local Councils.

The main difference between a letter and a memo is that for a memo there will be a range of specific formats that must be used. You need to discover the formats—or templates, and the internal rules for using them. You can find them on files in your Office, and every good Personal Assistant will have them.

Often, a memo will be used to provide information to staff, or to request an action, as well as to provide approval for an action or expenditure.

All the same Plain English principles for good writing apply to memos.

Collect copies of good memos and use them as starting points for your own memos.

The Report

The report is a distinctive kind of written communication.

More than any other form of written communication, the report is designed to provide information that will lead to some kind of decision by the reader.

It requires more preparation, has a broader range of external factors to consider, needs more follow up and demands better time management than do most other forms of written communication.

Reports fail for two main reasons:
- they provide information only, and
- the writer has not considered their audience

The writer who produces an effective report:

- is clear about their audience and what they want to them to do or know as a result of reading the report
- considers possible impacts or implications
- offers options or draws conclusions
- makes recommendations, (where to from here)
- communicates **all** these through the report

Good report writers apply the principles of Plain English described in the earlier chapter, but they also need to take some extra things into account.

Plan, Plan, Plan

A report is a project and needs to be planned and managed as you would any project.
Planning is crucial in producing a good report, and will always repay the time and energy you put into it.

You need to identify how you will make sure that you have all the information you need.
When writing a report, consider *why, what, who, where* and *how*:

- Why are you writing it?
- What is the topic about?
- What do you already know about it?
- Who else might know about it?

- Where might there be information about it?
- How do you make sure you are covering all the information?

Mind maps are excellent tools for the report writer:
1. To plan the project itself
2. To check with your boss or other key person that you are covering what is required
3. Once you have started your research, to plan your report itself

Cast your net wide when researching information. This can include people, libraries, the internet, other media, catalogues to find books, indexes to find periodical articles, bibliographies, search engines, interviews and focus groups, photographs, audio and video tapes or blogs.

Using a Draft

The draft is a valuable tool in gathering both information and support. It can be used to assess and sharpen your writing, to improve the range and quality of your information and options, and to gather support for your conclusions or recommendations.

Use a mind map to plan your draft.

You will need to consider the following:

- will you put out a draft for comment, before submission of your final report? Why? Who to? When?
- what if there are major challenges to your draft? What will you do with that information?
- have you addressed all the requirements of your brief or terms of reference?
- how will you organize your information and ideas?

The draft is also the time to check your spelling, grammar, layout and overall presentation.

While you need to do a proofing check of the draft yourself, it is good practice to ask someone to look at the document with fresh eyes. If you have been working on a report for some time, it will be so familiar that you can easily miss minor mistakes—or even the occasional glaring error or gap!

The Executive Summary

An Executive Summary can significantly improve your report. It may be the only part of your carefully crafted report that a busy person reads—so you need to make the best use of it.

In fact, research suggests that only 10 to 15 percent of reports are read in full—most people will only read the Executive Summary!

Your Executive Summary must engage and interest your reader—using all the Plain English principles. It is a concise description of the why, how and what of the Report.

Don't assume that your reader is familiar with your topic—you have spent some time researching, thinking and writing—others may not have had that opportunity. Your summary must engage and interest your reader.

Depending on the size of your report, the Summary could be between one and three pages long. It should include:
- key information
- possible impacts
- conclusions or options
- recommendations (*where to from here*)

As well, make sure you sign post your full report with clear headings, so that the reader of the Executive Summary can easily find their way if they need to follow up a point in the full report.

Plan the Finished Product

You need to think about the finished product early—the final format and presentation of the report is important.

Check your organization's conventions and report templates:
- what format will you use, for example will it be published in a booklet or online?
- how many copies? Distribution? Color? Cover? Binding?

- lead time for printing? Printed internally or externally?
- will there be a launch?
- do you need to make any formal acknowledgements?
- will you use appendices and attachments?
- how will you manage your bibliography, or sources consulted, or references?
- how will you present data such as tables, graphs, spreadsheets?
-

Doing the Writing

When you are writing a report, there is sometimes a temptation to fall back into the way you learned to write an essay or paper at school or university, i.e. academic writing.

Remember, day to day writing is about getting things done—you want your audience to know or do something.

If you don't want your report to be one that just sits on the shelf, gathering dust—then use all the Plain English techniques. This applies to all kinds of reports, including technical reports.

A useful technique is to structure your report in layers or tiers, for example:

- the Executive Summary— brief, one or two pages
- the main body of your report—the key points and discussion only
- Attachments—supporting details, particularly if you have a lot of technical data

A final point about report writing. Sometimes—because a report is often longer than letters or memos—we can tend to just keep on writing, and to put every piece of information we have discovered into it. Resist that temptation!

Checklist 3 will take you through each of the components of:
- What to consider
- Where to Start
- Scoping the Topic
- Finding the Information
- Putting the Information Together
- Implementation, Evaluation & Reflection

Job Applications, Covering Letters and Resumes

There are three parts to a job application:
- Resume
- Covering Letter
- Application

The essential principles in writing each of these start with the same ones for good letter writing:
- people dislike long resumes and applications
- you must give me a reason to read your resume or application—you must market yourself
- use Plain English

To these, you must add:
1. Study the organization that you want to work with—who are they, what do they do, what are their values, what kind of people do they employ now?
2. Find out what they want the successful applicant to actually do—get a job description if at all possible
3. Prepare some questions and then speak to the contact person

4. Be realistic—apply for jobs that you can do and that your background supports

Now you can start to prepare your job application and your customized resume!

Resume

The Resume is:

- a marketing document to get an interview
- your 15 second chance to impress the reader
- two to four pages of information relevant to the job
- a means of emphasizing relevant achievements, skills, abilities and experience
- a summary of the main elements of employment history, qualifications and personal details

It must be a document that reflects your own personal style. It must:

- make it easy for the reader to find information
- be 100% accurate in both the information supplied and the presentation and layout
- be concise

Keep your Resume short—think about your audience.

A good resume—that will be read and understood—will be no more than two to four pages long. Any longer and you run the very real risk that the reader will simply skim pages, or even skip most of them!

Wherever possible, you should make sure that your Resume is relevant to the job you are applying for. This does mean a little more work, but making sure that you are highlighting the experience and knowledge you bring to <u>this</u> particular job improves your chances of getting an interview.

Use Plain English, use lists and tables, focus on the key points and not on all the details. Remember—your resume needs to be interesting, short and easy to read.

Ask yourself:
- Who is my audience?
- What do I want them to know or do?
- Am I using Plain English?

Always tell the truth.

There is an example of a simple Resume format at the end of this book.

Note: Sometimes you will hear the term Curriculum Vitae or CV—this is another term for a Resume.

Covering Letter

The covering letter of your application is very important, as it may be the first information about you that the selection panel read. It is your first chance to market yourself!

Make sure that the covering letter clearly and concisely summaries your assertion that you are the right person for the position.

The letter should include the following:

- a reference to the advertisement for the job, including the position or job title
- a short statement that indicates that you are applying for the position, and that your application and resume are attached
- a short statement—no more than 10 to 15 lines—which tells them why you are the person for the job

Your Job Application

Your Application is a more detailed document, which specifically addresses the details of the job you are applying for. A good application will not be more than 4 to 6 pages long!

This is where you must demonstrate where you meet the job requirements with examples proving your competence in carrying out the specified duties.

One of the most effective ways to prepare your application is to use a Mind Map. Each of the selection criteria become the main branches, and the minor branches are how you can demonstrate your relevant experience, skills and knowledge.

It is vital that you consider your audience, and write for them. Most people interviewing for a job are busy, they have their usual everyday tasks to do. They want:

- something that is easy to read
- where they can quickly see how you might be able to meet each of the selection criteria—and that means you do NOT write 'see above'

Most job applications are really just to get you to the interview—and it is at the interview you must then persuade the employer that you are just the person for them.

In the interview you can add in all the extra details—put the flesh on your application.

And don't forget—your body language will be one of the most important components of whether your interview is successful or not. Make sure your appearance, your language, the way you look at the selection panel and so on work for you. This is something you should check out before your interview.

As with your resume, use all the Plain English techniques. Use lists and tables, focus on the key points and don't use jargon.

Example of a Resume Layout

Remember—your resume needs to be interesting, short and easy to read.
Ask yourself:

- Who is my audience?
- What do I want them to know or do?
- Have I made this resume relevant to the job I am applying for?
- Am I using Plain English?

Resume—Your Name

Name	
Company Name	(If appropriate)
Postal Address	
Telephone and Fax	
E-mail	
Web Site	(If appropriate)

Education Details

Include details of relevant academic qualifications, as well as any specific vocational skills such as computing skills, technical skills, etc

Professional Development

Include any short courses, forums, workshops, conferences, etc

Employment

This must only be a summary—most recent jobs first—and cover at least the past 10 years. Only include jobs more than 10 years ago if they are relevant to the job you are applying for, or if you have been in your current job for those 10 years. You only need to give the interviewer an **outline** of earlier jobs.

Use a table like this:

Jan .... to	Your Job Title, classification if appropriate.

present	organisation
.... to	
.... to	

Awards or Professional Recognition

Include any recognition, such as any civic awards, egg a Rotary scholarship, any sporting, Scouts or Rovers, creative arts, church or community awards, or any prizes or awards from any union, professional association or league.

Professional Associations or Memberships

Include details of any groups that you belong to that relate to your employment

Skills and Experience

Here you should summarise the key things that you have done, and then list them. Include any projects you have worked on, as well as everyday tasks. Use Plain English.

You might include brief details on:

- *Duties and responsibilities*
- *Career movement within company or organisation*
- *Achievements and successes*
- *Salary or job classification*
- *Reason for leaving—where appropriate*

Referees

Make sure you have spoken to them yourself before putting their names forward.

The Seven Secrets to Good Email

"Everyone gets so much information all day long that they lose their common sense"
Gertrude Stein 1874–1946

The Good and Bad of Email

It is hard now to envisage a world without email. Yet for many people it is only in the past few years that it has become an important means of communication.
Email has brought about extraordinary changes in working processes and habits, as well as how we communicate with family and friends.

It makes passing information around so easy—from a massive document sent across the world to a two line message sent to the person in the next desk or the next house.

It gives us access to people who in the past have been carefully guarded by secretaries and systems. It makes quick communication with large numbers of people possible.

And, as technology—such as mobile phones and tablets— becomes more affordable and simpler to operate, it allows a person to keep in contact—any time and from any where.

But it has its drawbacks as well:

- person to person communication can sometimes suffer
- it is estimated that between 25% to 40% of people's time at work can be taken up reading and answering emails
- there can be legal problems—from issues around formal contracts, industrial sabotage, conflict of interest, privacy and spamming through to harassment and discrimination
- security issues for Information Technology systems through introduced computer viruses
- your email can end up with anyone!

Email is a very specific form of communication—it is a quick, inexpensive and convenient way of communicating with a small or large audience, who may be next door or across the world.

It is great way to make arrangements—provided that they are not urgent. Instant delivery does NOT mean the recipient will read it immediately.

It is an excellent way to get information to a wide range of people—as long as your subject line is relevant or interesting enough to get them to read it.

It is a simple way of asking for a response—as a follow up, not as a long explanation and request for action.

It is a wonderful way to send information—as attachments not in the body of the email.

An email is not a letter, a report or the minutes of a meeting—but it is an excellent way of sending information to an audience, or asking for a response.

A crucial point to be aware of is: any email can end up anywhere with anyone! It is so easy:

- to put in the incorrect addressee
- to accidentally hit 'Reply to All"

- for the person who receives your email to send it to anyone

And it stays on the server, even if you delete it from your machine.

Remember: an email is a business document.

The 1st secret is: KEEP IT SIMPLE

Don't try and do too much with email.

Emails that are effective are those that keep it simple in the:
- subject line
- content—addressing only one topic
- language—using Plain English

If your email is longer than 3 or 4 paragraphs, then reconsider the format you are using. Would this communication be better sent as, for example, a letter or memo attached to the email?

And if you are using an attachment, then remember to actually attach it! A simple way to do this is to make the attachment as soon as you have written the Subject Line, before you start on the text of the email.

Clarify why you are writing the email, and who your audience is, as you would for any other form of communication.

Don't let it take the place of a face to face conversation.

So, don't write long, complex emails—not many people will read them!

Don't use fancy fonts, colored backgrounds, smileys and other distractions...they tend to make you look unprofessional.

The 2nd secret is: MAKE YOUR SUBJECT LINE RELEVANT & INTERESTING

People will read an email because of two things:
1. The addressee is one they want, need or expect to hear from
2. The subject line is relevant or interesting

We tend to consistently open only emails from a very select group of people—usually the boss, specific colleagues, particular friends, familiar businesses or accounts.

Otherwise, we will only open an email if the subject line persuades us to—it quickly tells us what it is about and why we should open it.

The first things your reader sees are who the email is from, and then the subject line.

Your subject line must be simple and clear, and make the reader want to read the email. If it doesn't, then the odds are that they will either delete it straight away, or leave it unread..."I'll look at that one later when I have time"...and of course, never get around to reading it.

The subject line needs to:
- tell you exactly what the email is about
- encourage you to make a quick decision about taking the next step and actually reading the email

Consider the following subject lines:

Poor Subject Lines	Good Subject Lines
Re: next meeting	Location for 1 April meeting
Re: minutes	Minutes & Action Plan from 1 April meeting

Which would you most probably open at once?

There are some more examples of Subject Headings at Annex B.

As an exercise, look at the emails you receive over the next week or so. Examine the subject lines and observe which ones:
- capture your interest, and why
- you probably wouldn't open and why not

Practice writing some yourself that quickly tell your audience what your email is about and why they should open it.

A good way to do this is to jot down, in dot point form, the answer to this question:
What do I want the reader to know or do?

Can the reader tell at once 'what's in it for them'? If the answer is yes—then you have your good subject line!

The 3rd secret is: THE TEXT SHOULD BE ONLY ONE SCREEN LONG

Generally, people prefer to read short sections of text on a screen.

Once an email starts to roll over onto a second screen, your reader is less likely to continue to read on—often they will scan ahead, and if the email looks as if it is a long one, they will simply delete it.

If you have more information than will fit on one screen, then send it as an attachment.

Use your email as the vehicle for sending the following kinds of document as attachments: DO NOT put the following information in the body of the email:

- a letter
- a report
- the agenda and minutes of a meeting
- an application
- a discussion paper

- a presentation

An exception to this rule is the 'series' email. Sometimes, a group of people with common interests or who work together will reply to each other in a series of emails. Each one includes all the previous emails—there may be a dozen emails in the chain.

This can be a useful technique if a group of people are exploring an issue or offering ideas or options as everyone can:
- follow the history of the topic
- see everyone else's input and comments

It can also lead to long, boring and confusing emails—use this technique sparingly.

If you have a message to send to the same addressees BUT it is on a new topic, then start a new email...don't add it to the chain.

The 4th secret is: STYLE & CONTENT

When you send an email from work, you must realize that it is a business document, in the same way as any business letter, memo or report. So—it should not be a casual document, full of personal comments.

Your email audience comes to your document asking **"Do I have to do anything?"** Good emails use a style and content that answers that question quickly and simply.

Use **Plain English**.

All good writing uses Plain English or Plain Language—clear writing which communicates as simply and effectively as possible. It:

- is written for the reader
- uses everyday English whenever possible
- uses a simple sentence structure—keep the sentence length down to an average of 15 to 20 words; one main idea in a sentence
- explains technical terms if necessary
- uses the active voice—'*We did it*', not '*It was done by us*'
- uses direct speech—'*We will*' not '*The Company shall*' This formal, disembodied voice talks past the reader
- directs the reader's eye: tables, lists, headings
- is concise
- uses words carefully and avoids unnecessary

- repetition or irrelevant words
- is positive—'We can pay you once you have signed the form' gets a much better response than 'We can't pay you unless you sign the form'

Keep your layout simple and clean—fancy fonts, colored backgrounds and bouncy graphics have their place—but it is NOT in emails.

Tables and dot points are a wonderful way of conveying information in an email—especially details of meetings, answers to queries and requests for information.

An email is not private. Your reader is able to broadcast an email widely, at the click of a button. Your email may end up being read by anyone or everyone. Are you prepared to have ANYONE, ANYWHERE, read what you have written?

As well, email is accessible on an organization's servers and on your ISP's servers if you use the Internet from home—in most cases even after you have deleted it from your computer.

Many places have rules about what can and can't be sent as email, i.e. bullying, harassment, pornography, incitements to violence, and regularly audit emails on servers.

Find out and comply with your company's policies on:
- security, privacy and confidentiality requirements
- virus checking requirements
- the use of disclaimers

- storage requirements
- the size of attachments
- deletion of emails
- record keeping requirements
- download limitations

The 5th secret is: TIME

Some people seem to assume that the speed of their email's transmission to someone else's computer should be matched by a lightning-like response time.

They don't consider:

- that the people they've emailed have their own lives and commitments other than checking for their emails
- the different time zones that the other person may live in

These days, many people manage their time by only reading their emails twice a day...consider the implications this habit has for your emails.

While it is important to answer email correspondence promptly—be realistic about deadlines...if you need an immediate answer, pick up the phone or physically visit the person.

The 6th secret is: MANAGE

Turn your email notification off, and set aside two or three periods during the day to deal with emails. The constant 'ting' of arriving emails breaks concentration, distracts your attention and it is just poor time management.

Set up folders in your email program, and regularly and often file emails into them.

Regularly delete emails that are no longer relevant.

As well, if you use electronic data management and filing systems, you will probably find that you will need to start filing emails onto the electronic system—in the same way that a piece of paper is filed in a file or cardboard folder.

The 7th secret is: EMOTION

When we write a letter or talk to someone on the telephone, we tend to be more careful about what we say, and how we say it, than when we write an email.

Email by its nature seems to encourage an immediate, instinctive, emotional response.

When this is combined with our tendency to be very informal in writing emails, then poor or even disastrous communication can happen.

If an email has upset you, made you angry or simply annoyed you, then certainly draft your answer. But don't send it yet. Follow these steps:

- GET UP, WALK AWAY for at least 10 minutes, then, re–read what you've written
- Ask yourself: 'What would be the impact if I said what I have written in this email to the addressee in person?"

If the answer is that you wouldn't say it, or it may make the situation worse—then redraft your email, or if you can, don't send the email but rather talk to the addressee directly.

Legal Issues

An email has the same legal status as a letter on your organization's letterhead.

Although an email appears to be an informal document, and in some people's minds is a 'virtual' document, in reality an email is a legal, business document.

Discussions, views, offers for contracts or work by email can be interpreted as representing the company or organization, and can be legally binding.

Don't harass or bully: don't send offensive material using email. The same rules that apply to speech and written communication regarding harassment, bullying and racial vilification apply to email. It is illegal.

SPAM is illegal in many countries.
Spam is the computer equivalent of junk mail and refers to unwanted email. Spam is often used to advertise products because of its low cost and potential to reach a large number of people.

It is mass email which is usually sent indiscriminately to hundreds or even hundreds of thousands of inboxes simultaneously.

Some SPAM is also sent maliciously, to annoy or harass the recipient—it can overload the recipient's inbox and even crash their computer.

There are two examples of good emails at **Annex C**

Checklist 1—Planning for writing

1. Why am I communicating—what do I want to happen?
2. What do I want my audience to know or do as a result of my communication?
3. Who is my audience?
4. Is it a single audience, or several audiences?
5. Who needs to know what? How and when do they need to know? How often?
6. What filters are operating? Mine, other people's?
7. How will I work with them?
8. What has been written before, can I learn from it? What form will I use—letter, memo, report, email?
9. How will I plan this—a mind map, a list
10. How will I check that the information has been received and understood?

Now, review some of your own writing—how might you have written them in the light of the questions in this Checklist?

What changes could you make? Try doing a redraft of your document.

Checklist 2—Improving your writing

1. Have I answered the question for the reader: What do they have to know or do and is that addressed early in the document?

2. How did I plan the content of my document? Did I start with a list of key points, or a mind map, or what else? What worked? What might I try next time?

3. Did I use appropriate headings? Did I use tables and lists? What could I try next time?

4. Did I keep to one idea in each sentence? Could I have put the points or headings in a different order?

5. Will the reader have enough information—too much?

6. Is all the information relevant? Is the material written in a logical flow? What could be moved to make better sense? What could have been left out?

7. Will I do a draft? Who will I get to look at it?

8. Does the body language of the document encourage reading and comprehension?

9. Do the formatting, layout, headings, white space, lists and tables direct the reader's eye?

10. Does the document give a context and encourage the reader to read the entire document? Will the audience have to ask for more information?

11. Am I using the active voice? Am I using 'you '? Am I using inclusive language?

12. What about jargon and simplicity? Is the writing clear and at an appropriate level?

13. If a decision is required, is it clear?

14. Have I used Plain English?

Now, review some of your own writing—how might you have written them in the light of the questions in this Checklist?

Checklist 3—Writing good reports

Part 1–Where to Start

1. Why am I writing this report?

   - is it to identify new approaches and ideas?
   - is it to assess a current project or program?
   - is it to recommend a new course of action?
   - is it to recommend a continuation?

2. Do I have a brief, or terms of reference? How do I clarify them?

3. Do I understand my audience(s)?

4. Who is my primary client or customer? Who are the stakeholders?

5. Who might be affected by the information I gain?

6. Who might support the report? Who might block the report? Why?

7. What are my timeframes?

8. What are my skills? Do I know how to write a report, make a presentation, etc?

9. Who can coach or mentor me?

10. How will I evaluate the project? What will the measures of success be?

Part 2—Scoping the report

1. What is this topic about? What? Why? How? Who? Where?
2. What do I already know about it? Who else might know about it?
3. Where might there be information about it?
4. Who has done some similar work before me?
5. Who can I talk to—or read, or listen to—to get an overview of the topic?
6. What form might the report be submitted in—a document, online, a presentation, etc?
7. How detailed a project plan do I need to set up?
8. Is there a budget that I need to manage?

Part 3—Finding the information

1. How might I structure the topic? Are there any immediately obvious headings?
2. Would a mind map help?
3. How do my terms of reference or brief define my structure?
4. How do I make sure I am covering all the appropriate ground?
5. How do I make sure I cover a range of opinions and approaches?
6. How do I look outside my own, individual, frame of reference?
7. Where do I find information? People, libraries, the internet, other media, etc.

8. What data collection methods will I use? e.g. interviews - structured or unstructured; group interviews and seminars; questions -- open-ended, closed or fixed choice; surveys; brainstorming, mind mapping; etc.

9. Issues to consider: sample size, questionnaire design, question design, language and cultural issues.

10. How will I document references and sources? e.g. professional association or discipline requirements; using footnotes and endnotes; Internet sources; etc).

Part 4—Putting the information together

1. How will I collect and manage my material (notes, information, keeping a running list of references and sources—where, from whom did information come from.

2. What filing system will I use? e.g. alphabetically, in a 2 ring folder; in a shoe box, etc.

3. What software will I use? e.g. Access, Excel, etc.

4. How will I organize my information and ideas?

5. How do I build the report? What will it look like, sound like, etc?

6. Drafts—will I put out a draft for comment, before submission of my final report? Why? Who to? When? What if there are major challenges? What will I do with that information?

7. Do I understand any Copyright, Privacy and Freedom of Information issues?

Part 5—Delivering the report

1. How will the report be delivered? To whom? Who needs copies?
2. Who will champion it?
3. Do I have the skills to present the report if necessary?
4. Where can I find out what I need to know about making a presentation?

Part 6— Implementation, Evaluation and Reflection

1. Where does the final product rest? Who else might want it?
2. How do I learn any lessons from this exercise? Reflecting, feedback, outcomes of implementation, etc.
3. What do I do with the 'lessons learned' information? e.g. new projects, training.

Annex A: Confusing Words Exercise

Find the words that are incorrectly used in this paragraph...there are about 16—yes 16—items to find...

"Its time you got some advise", the boss said, "their are too of you and the devise is starting to effect moral. In principal, all stationary should be kept over there, using the cabinet key's, not in that strange container".

I said "I thought its getting a bit personnel, and I will brake into it, and its they're fault if their's trouble".

PS: The answers are on the next page...

*"**It's** time you got some **advice**", the boss said, "**there** are **two** of you and the **device** is starting to **affect morale**. In **principle** all **stationery** should be kept over there, using the cabinet **keys**, not in that strange container".*
*I said "I thought **it's** getting a bit **personal**, I will **break** into it, and **it's their** fault if **there's** trouble".*

*("**Its** time you got some **advise**", the boss said, "**their** are **too** of you and the **devise** is starting to **effect moral**. In **principal**, all **stationary** should be kept over there, using the cabinet **key's**, not in that strange container".*

*I said "I thought its getting a bit **personnel**, and I will **brake** into it, and **its they're** fault if **their's** trouble").*

Explanation

- **Advice** is the noun (I will give you advice), **advise** is the verb (I will advise you)
- **There** means the place (Stand there, beside the desk), **there's** means the words have been shortened from there is (there's no need to do that right now), **their** means belonging to (their eyes are a lovely blue), **they're** means they are (with those lovely eyes, they're going to be beautiful when they grow up)
- **Too** – also, **two** – 2, **to** – toward (the two children are going to work after school too, as well as doing their homework, so that they can put some money to their school excursion fees next term)

- **Device** is the noun (a toaster is a device to toast bread), **devise** is the verb (I will devise a way to toast the bread even though our toaster is broken)
- **Effect** is the noun (tell us what effect the performance had on you), **affect** is the verb (the new policy will affect the everyday life of everyone)
- **Moral** means good or honorable (we expect moral behavior from our politicians), **morale** is the spirit or attitude (when politicians are dishonest, the community's morale plummets, and we feel bad)
- **Principal** means main or chief (the Principal of the school's principal interest is maintaining the high morals of the school), **principle** means rule, standard or the idea behind (the principle behind the school's rules is 'do as you would be done to')
- **Stationary** means standing still (if the ant stays stationary and doesn't get out of the anteater's way , it will be eaten), **stationery** means pens and paper and other similar office supplies (I will use my best stationery to write the obituary of the stationary ant)
- Adding the **'s** to a noun means that the word owns the subject, or that the words have been shortened (the cabinet's keys open only that

particular cabinet; there's no way that we can do that), adding the **s** to a noun makes the noun plural (one cabinet, two cabinets)

- **Its** means belongs to (the cabinet has its own unique keys), **it's** means the words have been shortened from it is (it's a real nuisance when someone misplaces the keys to the cabinet)
- **Personnel** means a group of workers (the Unit's personnel are all employed under the same working conditions), **personal** means private (my medical records are personal, and I don't want anyone else to see them)
- **Brake** means stop – it can be either a noun or a verb (I pulled on the brake in my car to try and brake the motion of the car), **break** means to split or smash or the result of smashing – it too can be a noun or verb (I used a stone to break the windscreen of the car, and it caused a jagged break right down the middle)

Annex B: Email Subject Lines

Poor Subject Lines	Good Subject Lines
Computer System Virus Information	New computer virus alert
Goods supplied	Urgent invoice attached for payment
Instruction in Sales	Nominate NOW for the new Sales workshop
Anticipated changes in technical innovations to complex voice recognition equipment availability	When to obtain your new voice recognition dictation equipment

Poor Subject Lines	Good Subject Lines
Re: Roster	Revised roster for April
Invitation	Lunch invitation for next week
Next meeting	Guest speaker for next meeting
Comments needed on updated procedure by Monday	Last chance to comment on updated procedure
Discount period finishes soon	You still have a chance to get the discount, but only until noon TODAY

Annex C: Example of a Good Email

Here are two options of an email telling a team about changes to a piece of software they all use. You want them to know:

- what they must do and when
- that everyone has had input
- that the system meets legislative requirements
- training is available

Each Option uses Plain English techniques, i.e.:

- it tells the audience :*'what's in it for me'*
- uses an interesting subject line
- uses tables
- uses dot points
- uses positive language
-
- Note: While both Options are very clear, you can see how much simpler it is to read and use the first Option— with its table and dot points!

Option 1

To: All Staff Members
Subject Line: IMS: Start Date and Requirement for New Password

The upgrade of the Department's Information Management System **(IMS)** is complete, and the new system will go live on **1 July**.

On 1 July, <u>everyone</u> will need to the following:

Steps	Action
1	Log onto IMS
2	Enter your current password
3	Change your password to a new one **with at least 8 characters— consisting of six letters and 2 numbers**

We strongly recommend that you make sure **<u>to log onto IMS as the first computer application you open</u>** each time you turn your computer on—this will speed your computer up.

Two hour training sessions are available. Please contact the IMS team: **ims@.....** to arrange a session.

Your input was important in the upgrade process, and we hope you enjoy the improved System.

IMS Team

Option 2

To: All Staff Members
Subject Line: IMS: Start Date and Requirement for New Password

The upgrade of the Department's Information Management System **(IMS)** is complete, and the new system will go live on **1 July**.

The new system meets the legislative requirements, and as well, your comments were taken into account as the system was updated.

You are required **to enter a new password to access any data**. The password must contain at least 8 characters— consisting of six letters and 2 numbers. Once you have entered this password, you will be able to access your documents.

For ease of use, we strongly recommend that you make sure to log onto IMS as the first computer application you open each time you turn your computer on.

Two hour training sessions are available. Please contact the IMS team: **ims@.....** to arrange a session.

We hope you enjoy the improved System.

IMS Team

Author Profile

J H Hood has a Bachelor of Arts, a Diploma in Education and the National Medal. She has extensive experience across government, the private sector and community organizations: as a senior manager as well as training adults in the workplace in a wide range of management and personal skills.

She has worked with many thousands of people, helping them to build the skills to survive and thrive in the workplace. Feedback on her training and coaching focuses on how practical her material is, and how quickly positive outcomes come from using it.

The 'How To" series comes form her love of writing and her experience helping people build their skills and knowledge.

She and her partner live in the foothills of Adelaide, where they can watch koalas climbing the tree outside her study window. Their two cats don't even stir!

The delightful graphics are by Mal Briggs:
http://www.impactcomics.com.au

You might find another in this "How to" series useful:

How to Book of Meetings: Conducting Effective Meetings

Have you just been asked to chair a meeting, or take the minutes, or set up a meeting agenda? Need some help? Would samples of an agenda or minutes be useful? What about some techniques for chairing a meeting or dealing with difficult people? Then this 60 page "How to" book is for you.

In it you will find:

- how to decide whether there should be meeting
- how to set up the agenda
- the importance of setting timeframes in the agenda—and sticking to them
- how to make sure that time is not wasted and the important items are covered
- how to chair the meeting
- how to stop time wasters and to make sure you spend the right time on the right topics
- how the minute taker can collect the right information during the meeting
- how to write the minutes
- how to get the best out of the participants
- how to deal with difficult people

There are also:

- a checklist for the meeting chair
- agenda example and agenda template
- minutes example and minutes template
- a checklist for how to improve your meetings
- a checklist for getting the best out of people
- a checklist for the minute taker
- a checklist for dealing with disagreements, differences and conflict

Turn your meetings into ones that:

- are packed with all the right information
- make excellent decisions
- foster good team work

There are more in the "How to" series on the way.

CPSIA information can be obtained at www.ICGtesting.com
Printed in the USA
BVOW01s2224290913

332475BV00014B/278/P